The WINE *Journal*

The WINE *Journal*

Jennifer McCartney

Skyhorse Publishing

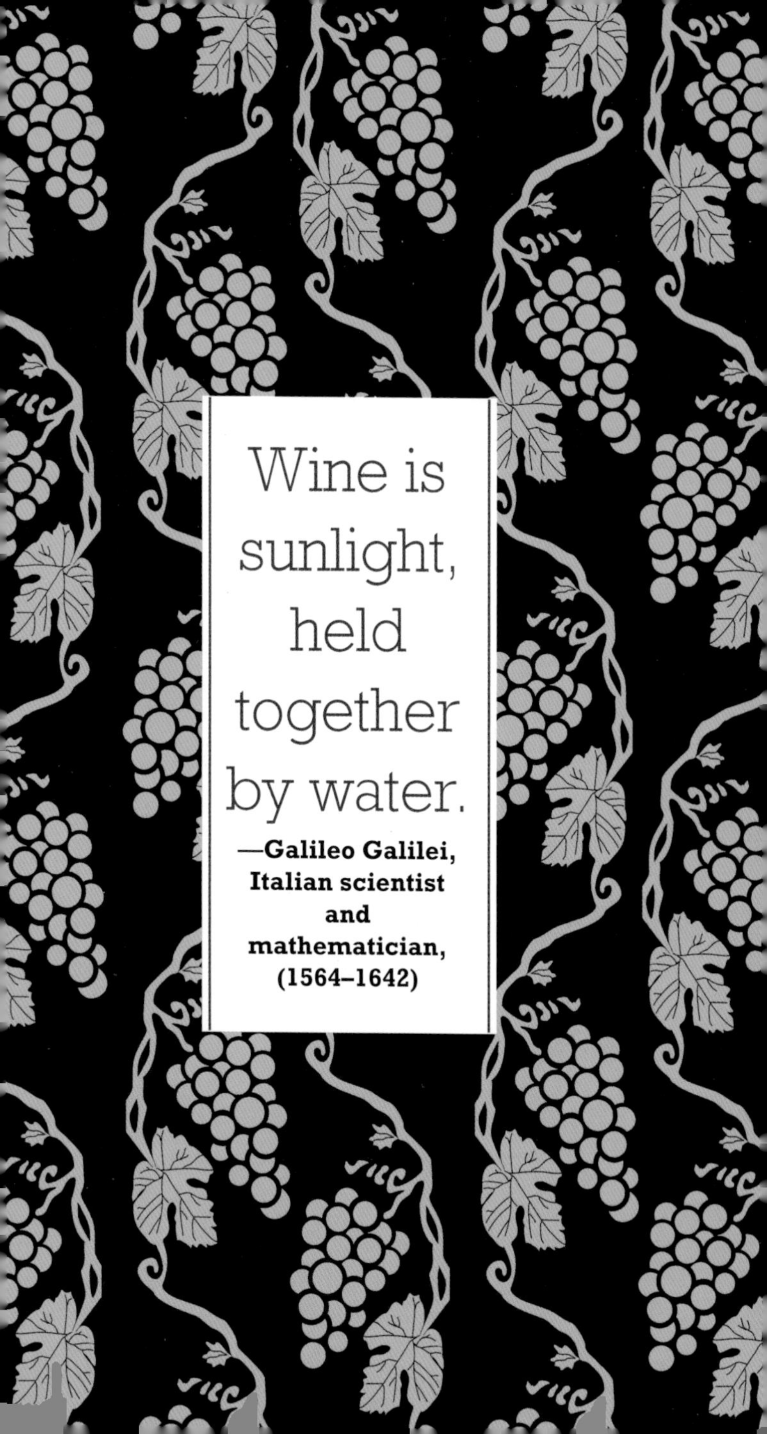

Wine is sunlight, held together by water.

—Galileo Galilei, Italian scientist and mathematician, (1564–1642)

WITH SPECIAL THANKS TO
ALEX PALMER

Skyhorse Publishing books may be purchased in bulk at special discounts for sales promotion, corporate gifts, fund-raising, or educational purposes. Special editions can also be created to specifications. For details, contact the Special Sales Department, Skyhorse Publishing, 555 Eighth Avenue, Suite 903, New York, NY 10018 or info@skyhorsepublishing.com.

www.skyhorsepublishing.com

10 9 8 7 6 5 4 3 2 1

Library of Congress Cataloging-in-Publication Data available on file.
ISBN: 978-1-61608-072-3

Printed in China

Contents

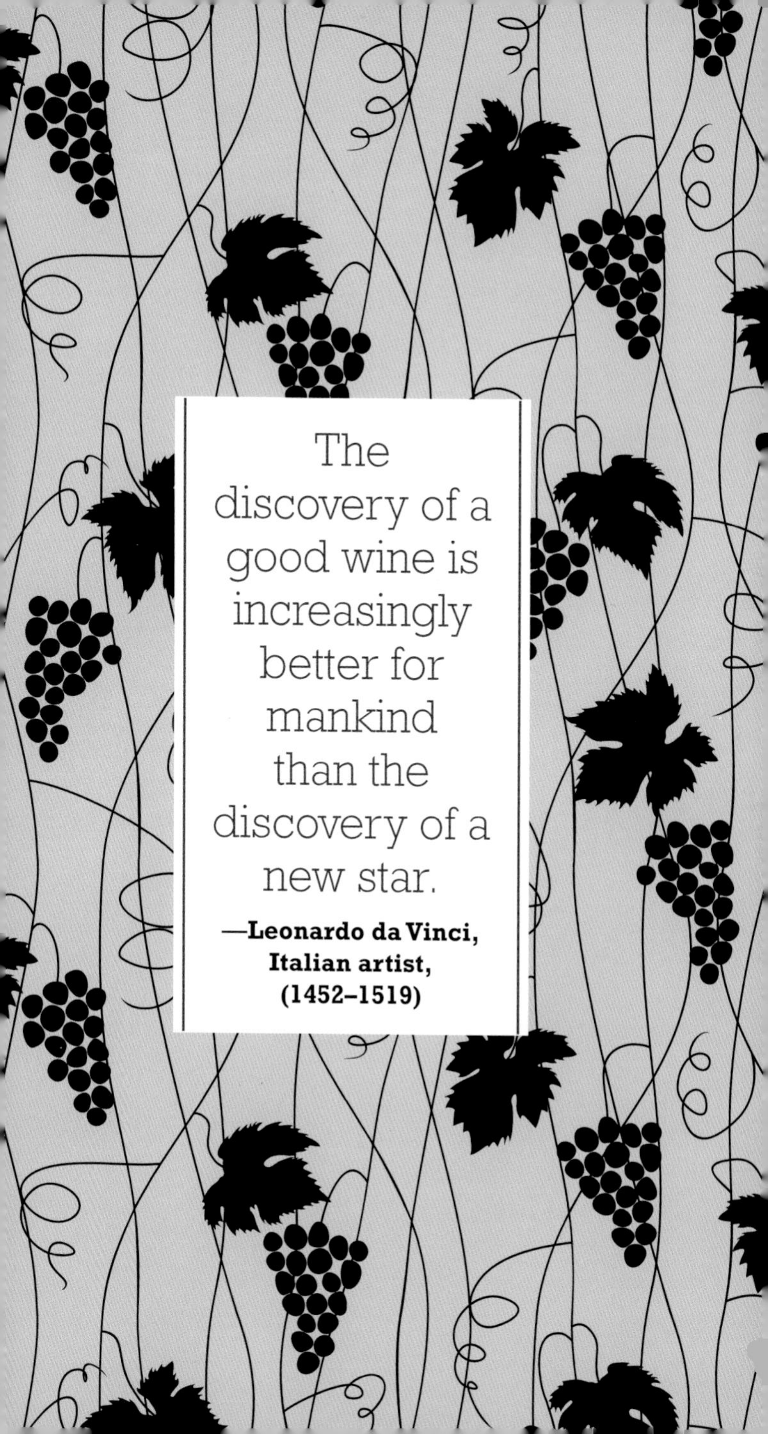

The discovery of a good wine is increasingly better for mankind than the discovery of a new star.

—Leonardo da Vinci, Italian artist, (1452–1519)

Introduction

Too often wine intimidates more than it invites. Caricatures of wine snobs and exacting rules about the proper ways to pour, swirl, and sip can smother the simple fun of drinking a fine vintage. Whether raising a glass with friends or enjoying solitary sips over a good book, we find far more pleasure in interacting with wine on our own terms and in our own words.

This journal aims to help you put those words down on paper, to make drinking wine about you and your experiences as much as about details of grape variety and vintage. As you observe and note each encounter with a red, white, or rosé, you will continually build a string of fond (and occasionally unpleasant) memories you can revisit months and years later. Your entries will allow you to capture how your palate develops and experiences broaden, turning a glass of wine into an enriching and personal venture.

So uncork the bottle and prepare to enjoy.

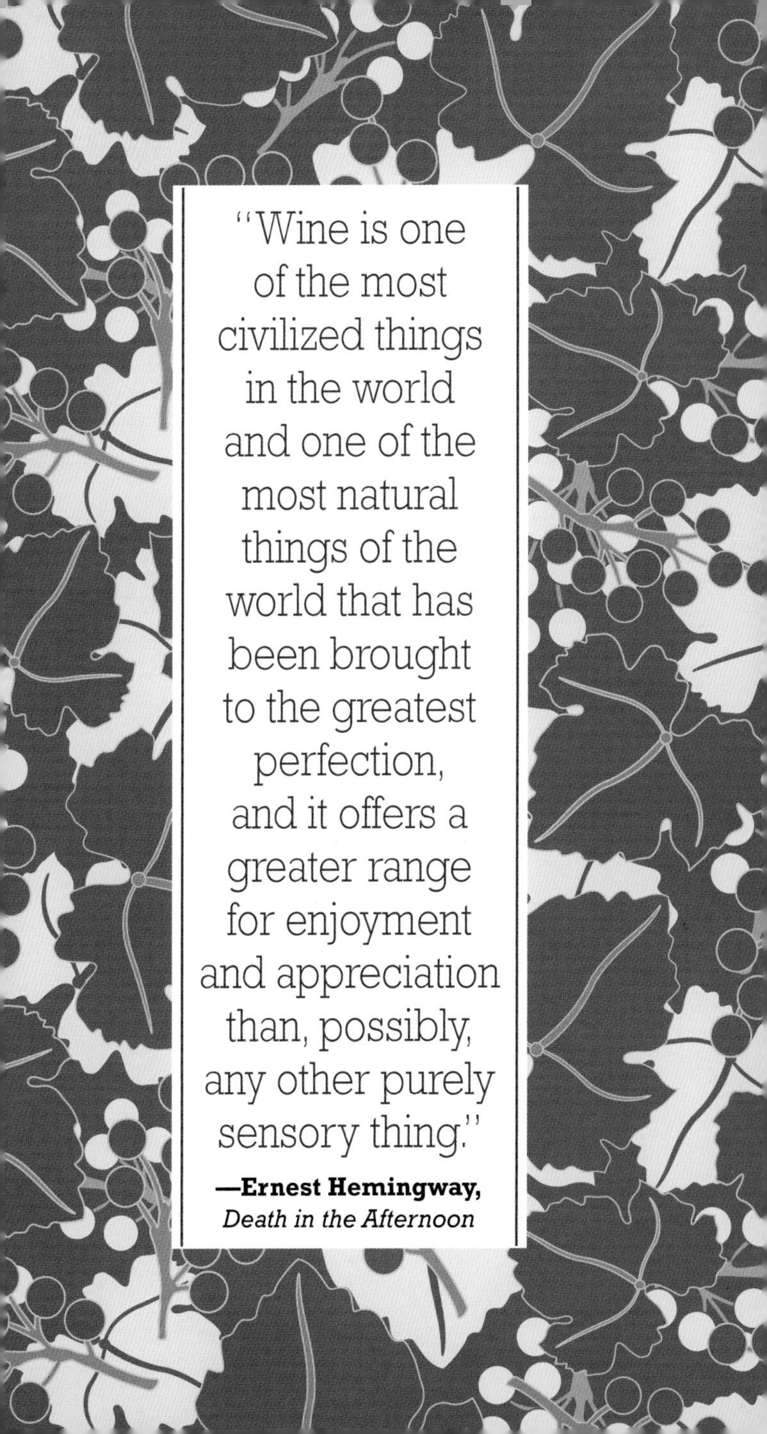
"Wine is one of the most civilized things in the world and one of the most natural things of the world that has been brought to the greatest perfection, and it offers a greater range for enjoyment and appreciation than, possibly, any other purely sensory thing."
—Ernest Hemingway,
Death in the Afternoon

Some Tips as You Begin

For beginners as well as regular wine drinkers, these are some basic suggestions on how to get the most out of a wine-drinking experience.

Getting Started

Before you even open the bottle, be sure the wine is at the proper temperature. If it's white, chill it in the refrigerator for an hour or more before serving. If it's red, serve it at room temperature, or better yet, at "cellar temperature" (55–63°F).

Make sure you have the proper accessories as well—put down the Swiss Army knife corkscrew and use a quality opener for a quality bottle of wine. Use larger glasses for reds to better appreciate their complexities, smaller ones for whites to help keep the liquid cool, and narrow flutes for sparkling wine to preserve the bubbles.

"It's my firm belief that wine is enhanced by experience. You may have a bottle that is rated poorly, but pair it with the right food, company, and atmosphere, it may be one of the most memorable bottles ever. I think people will enjoy wine a lot more if they take a little of the 'serious' out of it."—***Laura Mohseni, General Manager of the winery division at Riverbench Vineyard and Winery in Santa Maria, CA.***

If a bottle has been sitting on the shelf for a while, wipe the top with a cloth to remove any dust or residue. Inspect the top of the cork for mold or discoloration—if you find that any appears only at the top, simply wipe it off as well.

Once you remove the cork from the bottle, give the wine a sniff. Not only does this give you an aromatic preview of what you are about to enjoy, you can also ensure there are no unpleasant notes that may indicate spoilage.

Eyes and Nose

Pour yourself a glass, filling it about halfway, and let it breathe for a moment. Especially for reds and select whites, this allows the wine to mingle with the air, releasing its aromas and mellowing out, improving the overall flavor. Generally, 15–20 minutes of breathing time is ideal, though some wines may open up with more time—an hour for young reds, and 2–3 hours for old, fine reds is not a bad idea. You might consider decanting these (pouring the wine into a large liquid container like a pitcher or flower vase).

Note the appearance of the wine, including its cloudiness or clarity, density and sediment. The appearance indicates its body (or weight) as well as the strength of the alcohol. Examine the color by holding the glass at about a 45-degree angle, ideally in front of a white wall or tablecloth.

"Go around to the grocery store and smell everything in the produce section, smell the spice rack. That's how you will be able to develop your 'smell vocabulary' as I call it. If you haven't smelled something a couple times, you are not going to have that reference point." ***—Laurie Forster, national speaker and author, known as The Wine Coach.***

The color of the wine comes from the skin of the grapes. While the juice from both red and white grapes is white, when the skins of red grapes are left in during fermentation, the pigment from the skin leeches out, coloring the wine (when red grape skins are removed, it creates a *blanc de noirs*, or "white wine from red grapes"). The antioxidant tannins contained in the skin also leech out during fermentation, giving reds their more acidic taste and cancer-fighting attributes. Color does not relate to the flavor of the wine, but can indicate its age. White wines develop a deeper color as they age, while reds grow paler.

Swirl the wine in the glass and note the ring of liquid and dripping lines coming down from it. These are the legs (or alternately the tears, fingers, church windows, or curtains). Wine is a mixture

"There are no hard rules. A cloudy wine can taste delicious, and a beautiful, colored sample might not. If you happen to know the wine, the visual aspect can be a lot more informative, as you can compare the current wine with previous bottles you tasted." ***—Paul David, Founder of Wine Pairings, a wine concierge service based in Denver, CO.***

of alcohol and water, and the alcohol, which has a lower surface tension and faster evaporation rate than water, goes up the side of the glass as it evaporates. Due to the film of water on top, the alcohol arches up, and the water's surface tension increases, then breaks, causing the water to form beads that drip down the glass. Though some consider the legs indicators of the wine's quality, it merely points to its alcohol content: lots of legs mean lots of alcohol.

Continue to swirl the glass to expose the wine to air and help release its full bouquet. Inhale the smell, or nose, of the wine. To best take in the aroma, put your nose fully into the glass as you lift it to your face, breathing in deep, quick bursts and inhaling slightly with your mouth as well. Observe the various scents you detect, such as cherries from pinot noir, black currants from cabernet sauvignon, or apples from chardonnay. Can you smell smoke or wood or soil? Is it fruity or floral?

It is important to focus on the nose of the wine first, as it plays a major part in how we experience the taste when we actually drink the wine.

"Don't like what you smell? Log it in your brain by coming up with a few descriptions for it. A few common aromatic descriptors that can give away major faults are wet cardboard, stale dishwater, and Band Aid. Don't be afraid to learn from wine professionals, such as sommeliers at restaurants, by asking their opinion." ***—Conor McCormack, resident Winemaker at Brooklyn Winery.***

Touch and Taste

Now, finally, taste the wine. Take a sip and hold it in your mouth for a moment, and note several elements as it moves across your tongue. You will notice sweetness on the tip of the tongue, saltiness and acidity on the sides (in the front and the back, respectively), and bitterness, particularly from the wine's tannin content, at the back.

Just as you opened your mouth slightly to take in the wine's nose, utilizing your nasal receptors in the olfactory bulb is crucial to fully experiencing the flavor in your mouth (just see what happens to the taste when you hold your nose and sip). As you breathe in through your mouth, the wine will vaporize—allowing you to take in the aroma.

Notice the weight and the size of the wine known as the wine's body. A lighter wine, like Riesling moves quickly across the palate, while a full-bodied one like Chardonnay feels heavier.

Also observe the mouthfeel, or texture of the wine. It may have a coarse feel, if there is a high

"You do not have to be a scholar or wine expert or know anything technical about wine to simply enjoy it and therein lies the beauty, the truth, of wine: Wine is many things but mostly it is time travel in a bottle and liquid art." ***—Malia Milstead, Wine Director for the Agora in Washington, DC, and winner of the 2009 Wine Spectator Best of Excellence award for her work as Wine Director of The Source by Wolfgang Puck.***

acidity in whites or high tannin count in reds. Low amounts of these elements will create a softer feel. A dry wine, with little or no sugars left after fermentation (what some call "fermented right out"), is the opposite of a sweet wine, which is generally enjoyed as a dessert wine after meals. For describing mouthfeel, fabric terms can be useful, such as "rough" like flannel or "smooth" like silk.

After swallowing the wine, take note of the finish—the taste it leaves in your mouth. Higher quality wines generally leave a balanced taste and a long finish. Consider counting from one to ten to see how long you taste the wine to determine whether it has, say, a five-second or an eight-second finish.

When pairing wine with food, sip the wine and note the taste and finish both before and after tasting the food. The contrast will illuminate how they compliment and interact with one another.

Finally, take in the many other aspects of the wine-drinking experience that may not have to do with what's in your glass. How is the atmosphere and company shaping your experience? What thoughts or associations occur to you that may have little to do with the wine itself? Just as you let the wine breathe, let your mind relax and open up. Drink in the moment and see where it takes you.

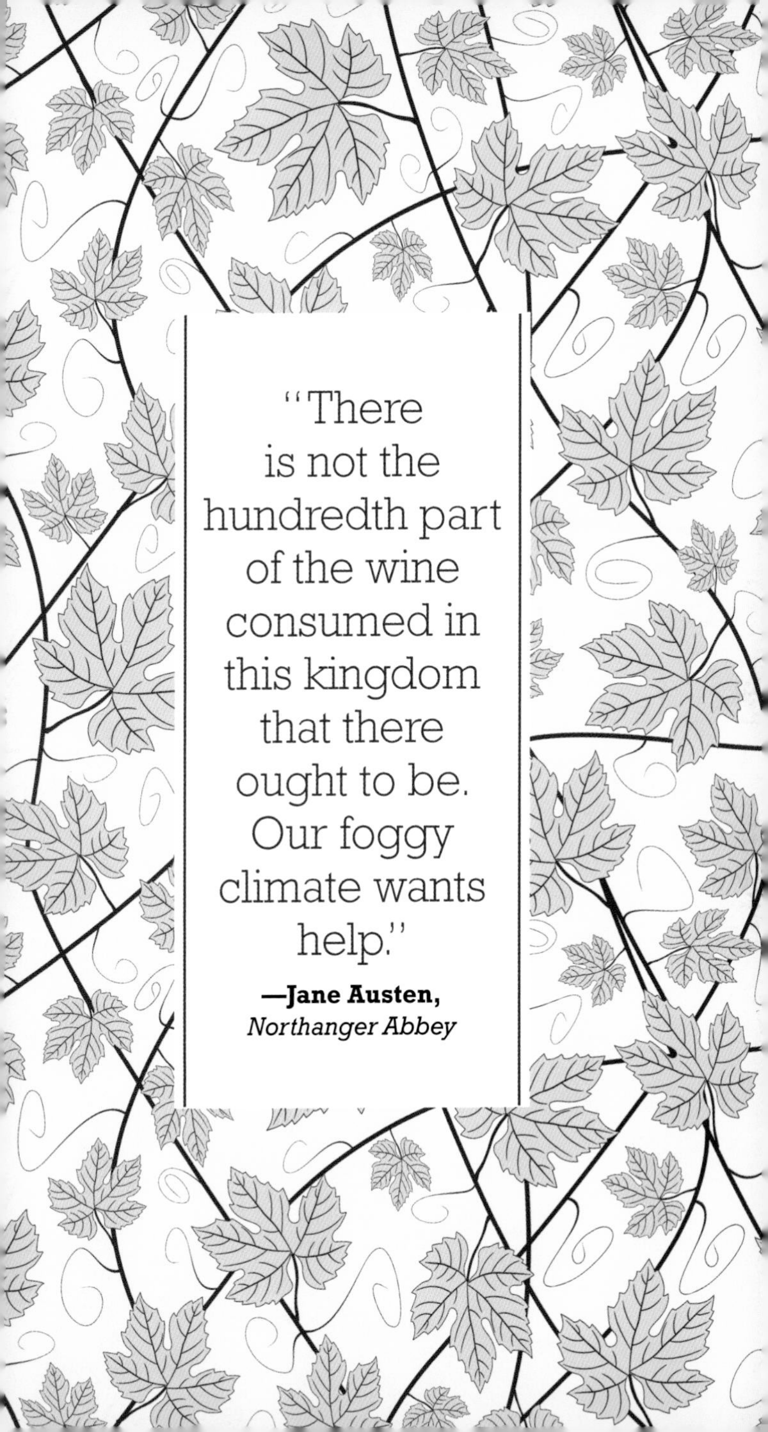
"There
is not the
hundredth part
of the wine
consumed in
this kingdom
that there
ought to be.
Our foggy
climate wants
help."
—Jane Austen,
Northanger Abbey

Winemaking Made Easy

The process of making wine is inherently simple:

- Pick some grapes
- Squeeze the grapes
- Put the juice in a container
- Wait

The complexities of winemaking arise from the thousands of possible variables contained within these four steps. Where are the grapes planted? What's the soil like? Is it a dry climate or a temperate one? What variety are the grapes? What sort of container will you store the liquid in? An oak barrel or a plastic bucket in your basement? How long will you wait before you drink it? Five years? Three weeks?

Each of these variables affects the sort of wine that is eventually produced. To learn all about the winemaking process, try visiting a local winery or taking the time to stop at one on your next road trip or vacation. You can learn a lot from wandering the vineyards, tasting the wines, and talking to the people who make them.

Wine Myths and Facts

Older is better. While certain wines need time to age well, no amount of aging will make a bad wine better.

Expensive wine is better wine. These days there are thousands of wineries all over the world—many of them committed to bringing excellent wine to the masses. Many wonderful bottles of wine are available at reasonable prices.

You should listen to the experts. While learning about wine from those "in the know" can be an important part of your wine education, only *you* know what you really like.

Screw cap lids are only used on cheap wine. Many wineries use screw caps on their best wines to avoid them being spoiled by a bad cork. This isn't a reliable way to tell if a wine is "good."

Always drink white wine with white meat and red wine with red meat. While a crisp white wine can enhance the flavor of a light-tasting fish, it's okay to switch it up any way you like. Red wine can go well with salmon, for example—and pizza tastes good with just about anything.

Did you know? By acreage, grape vineyards are the world's number one crop—more than 20 million acres.

Did you know? Ice wine is made from grapes that are left to freeze on the vine. Canada is the world's largest producer of ice wine.

Did you know? In the 1940s in Napa Valley, California, the primary fruit crop was prunes.

Did you know? There are over 10,000 varieties of wine grapes worldwide.

Did you know? When Viking Leif Ericsson landed in North America in 1001 A.D., he was so impressed by the proliferation of grapevines that he named it *Vinland*. The Vikings made good use of the grapes: excavations at the archeological site L'Anse a Meadows in Newfoundland and

Labrador show that the Vikings were the first to make wine in North America.

Did you know? There is at least one commercial winery in every American state, including Hawaii and Alaska! There is also at least one commercial winery in each of the ten provinces in Canada!

Wine Glossary

acidity: Refers to the tartness in a crisp wine.

aeration: When a wine is exposed to oxygen to soften and improve its flavors. Aeration can be achieved by either uncorking the bottle or using a decanter to hasten the process.

Angel's share: The portion of a wine in an aging barrel that is lost to evaporation.

aroma: The fragrance of the wine's grapes, particularly associated with young wines.

balance: When no single element overpowers another, a wine is balanced.

blending: The combination of two different wines by winemakers to produce a consistent finished wine.

body: Indicates the richness and fullness of a wine, ranging from light-, to medium-, to full-bodied.

Bordeaux: The region in Southwest France distinguished by the quality of wine produced in many of its districts.

bouquet: Describes the complex aromas of mature wines.

brut: A French term describing dry champagnes or extremely dry sparkling wines.

cabernet sauvignon: The best known and most popular of the red wine grapes, it can grown almost anywhere and still produce excellent dry, full-bodied, and complex wine.

champagne: Either a white sparkling wine produced in the Champagne region within France's Marne Valley or a generic name for sparkling wines.

chaptalization: The highly controlled and, in some parts of the world, illegal process of adding sugar to the wine before or during fermentation to increase alcohol levels.

chardonnay: The most popular of all the white grapes, produces rich, oaky medium- to full-bodied wines.

complex: A wine with a variety of odors, nuances, and flavors.

corked: Wine with an unpleasant taste and stale flavor, caused by moldy corks and occurring in approximately 5 percent of all bottles.

demi-sec: A French term meaning "half-dry." It was originally used to describe a dry Champagne, but it is now used to describe a sweet sparkling wine.

dry: A taste closely associated with tannins, occurring when most of the sugar in a wine has been converted to alcohol.

finish: The final impression of lingering flavors and sensations after a wine is swallowed.

fruity: Describes wines that exhibit rich smells and flavors of fresh fruit, often grapes, but sometimes of apples, berries, or others.

fortified: Wine to which a distilled spirit has been added, increasing the alcohol level to nearly double that of most table wines. Commonly known fortified wines include Madeira, Marsala, port, and sherry.

lees: Wine sediment that occurs during and after fermentation, and consists of dead yeast, grape seeds, and other solids. Wine is separated from the lees by racking.

legs: The tracks of liquid that cling to the sides of a glass after the contents have been swirled. It is often said that the thicker the legs, the higher the alcohol content.

merlot: A red wine grape originally grown in Bordeaux and now grown worldwide. It is often used to soften cabernet sauvignon, but merlot is also very popular in the United States as a smooth, rich, fruity red wine low in tannins.

mouthfeel: The way a wine feels in the mouth, not to be confused with taste.

Nappa Valley: The most famous winemaking region in America, located in Northern California, chiefly known for its exports of cabernet sauvignon, chardonnay, merlot, and pinot noir.

N.V.: Nonvintage, or a wine made from grapes harvested in different years commonly found in sparkling wines.

pinot blanc: A white wine grape producing dry, fresh wines in Alsace, California and northern Italy.

pinot noir: A red wine grape said to date back to as early as the first century. It is predominantly found in Burgundy though also grown in regions of Oregon, California's Russian River Valley, and Santa Barbara. It produces superior fruity, complex wines.

port: Sweet, dark-red dessert wine originally from Portugal's Douro Valley. It ranges in prices depending on the wine's maturity.

racking: The process of drawing wine off the sediment, such as lees, after fermentation and moving it into another vessel.

rosé: Pink wines that are produced from the shortened contact of red wine juice with its skins, reducing the red color of the wine. These wines can also be made by blending a small amount of red wine with white wine.

rough: The sensation one experiences with very astringent wines.

spicy: A tasting term used to note odors and flavors reminiscent of various aromatic spices that are found in certain wines.

sweet: Wines with perceptible sugar content on the nose and in the mouth.

table wine: Generally, any wine that is not sparkling or fortified. In the United States, these wines must also be between 7 and 14 percent alcohol by volume.

tannins: The substances from the grape that give wine its astringent quality, leaving a bitter, dry, puckery aftertaste.

terroir: French for "soil," this term refers to the highly-valued geographical conditions of a vineyard, which affect the characteristics of the resulting wine.

unoaked: Also known as unwooded, refers to wines that have been matured without contact with wood/oak such as in aging barrels.

varietal: A wine made principally from one grape that carries the name of that grape.

vermouth: Any of several white wines flavored with aromatic herbs, either dry and used as an aperitif, or sweet in cocktails.

vertical and horizontal wine tasting: In a vertical tasting, different vintages of the same wine type from the same winery are tasted. This emphasizes differences between various vintages. In a horizontal tasting, the wines are all from the same vintage but are from different wineries. Keeping wine variety or type and wine region the same helps emphasize differences in winery styles.

vigneron: French for vine grower.

vin: French for wine.

vinification: The process of making wine.

vintage: The year a wine was bottled or the grapes were harvested.

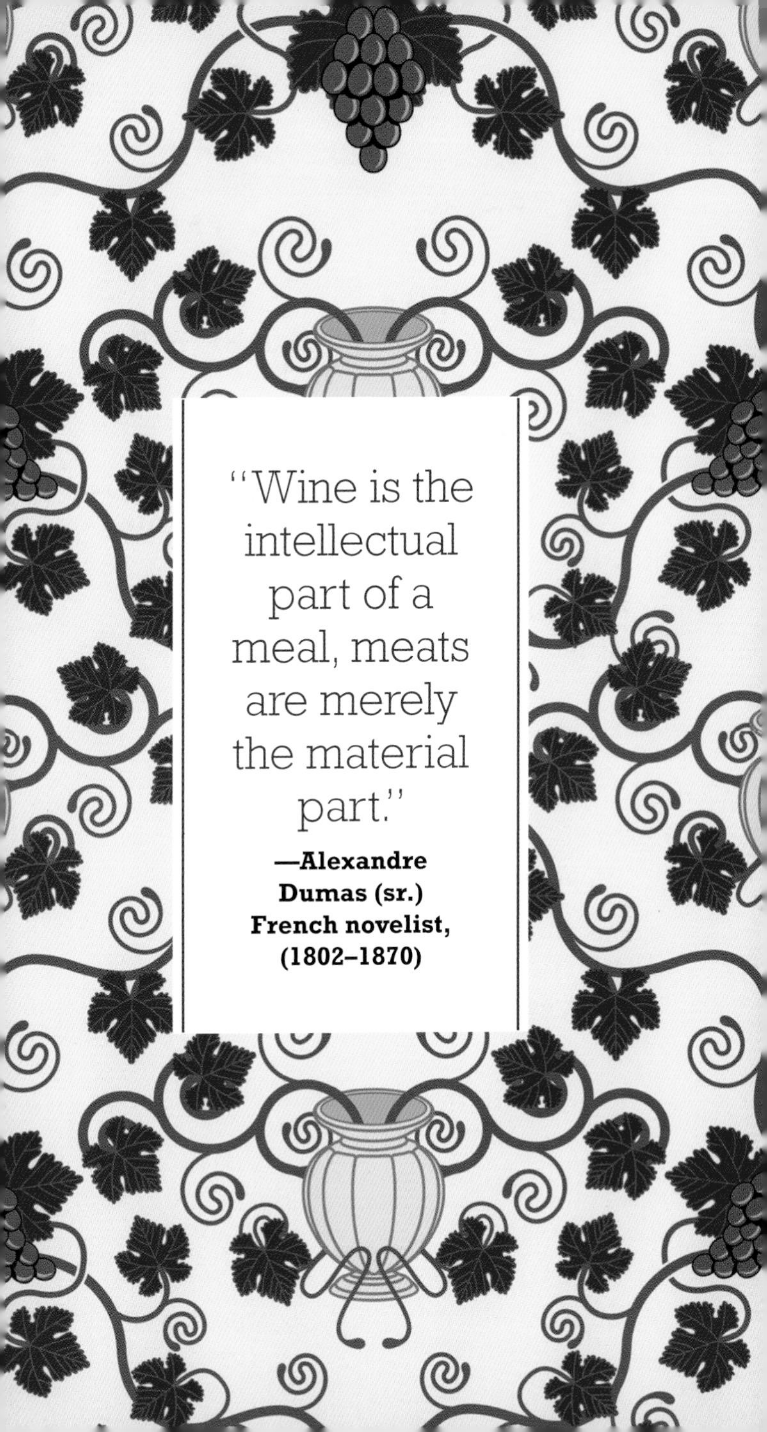
"Wine is the intellectual part of a meal, meats are merely the material part."
—Alexandre Dumas (sr.) French novelist, (1802–1870)

Wine Name | Price

S. A. Prüm
Vine Yard 15.99

Tasted where and when:
Blue slate
Riesling Kabinett
Estate Bottled

Vintage:
2007

Country: Germany
Region:
Mosel River Valley

Comments:

Shared with:
good riesling

Served with:

Overall Rating: | | | | | | | | | |

Wine Name	Price
gustav adolf schmitt vineyard	11.99

Tasted where and when: Wiersteiner name Rehbach

Vintage: 209

Country: germany

Region: Rheinhessey

Comments: spätlese Riesling

Shared with:

Served with: good

Overall Rating: | | | | | | | | | | |

Wine Name	Price

Tasted where and when:

Vintage:

Country:

Region:

Comments:

Shared with:

Served with:

Overall Rating: | | | | | | | | | | |

Wine Name	Price
	)

Tasted where and when: 14.99

Vintage: 2006

Country: German
Region: Kues

Comments: Cardinal Cusanus Stiftswein
Bernkasteler Badstube
Riesling Hochgewächs
Trocken
Mosel

Shared with:

Served with:

Overall Rating: | | | | | | | | | | |

Wine Name	Price

Tasted where and when:

Vintage:

Country:

Region:

Comments:

Shared with:

Served with:

Overall Rating: ☐☐☐☐☐☐☐☐☐☐

Wine Name	Price

Tasted where and when:

Vintage:

Country:

Region:

Comments:

Shared with:

Served with:

Overall Rating:

Wine Name	Price

Tasted where and when:

Vintage:

Country:

Region:

Comments:

Shared with:

Served with:

Overall Rating: | | | | | | | | | | |

Wine Name	Price

Tasted where and when:

Vintage:

Country:

Region:

Comments:

Shared with:

Served with:

Overall Rating:

Wine Name	Price

Tasted where and when:

Vintage:

Country:

Region:

Comments:

Shared with:

Served with:

Overall Rating: | | | | | | | | | | |

Wine Name	Price

Tasted where and when:

Vintage:

Country:

Region:

Comments:

Shared with:

Served with:

Overall Rating: ☐☐☐☐☐☐☐☐☐☐

Wine Name	Price

Tasted where and when:

Vintage:

Country:

Region:

Comments:

Shared with:

Served with:

Overall Rating: | | | | | | | | | | |

Wine Name	Price

Tasted where and when:

Vintage:

Country:

Region:

Comments:

Shared with:

Served with:

Overall Rating: | | | | | | | | | | |

Wine Name	Price

Tasted where and when:

Vintage:

Country:

Region:

Comments:

Shared with:

Served with:

Overall Rating: | | | | | | | | | | |

Wine Name	Price

Tasted where and when:

Vintage:

Country:

Region:

Comments:

Shared with:

Served with:

Overall Rating: | | | | | | | | | | |

Wine Name	Price

Tasted where and when:

Vintage:

Country:

Region:

Comments:

Shared with:

Served with:

Overall Rating:

Wine Name	Price

Tasted where and when:

Vintage:

Country:
Region:

Comments:

Shared with:

Served with:

Overall Rating: | | | | | | | | | | |

Wine Name	Price

Tasted where and when:

Vintage:

Country:

Region:

Comments:

Shared with:

Served with:

Overall Rating: | | | | | | | | | | |

Wine Name	Price

Tasted where and when:

Vintage:

Country:

Region:

Comments:

Shared with:

Served with:

Overall Rating:

Wine Name	Price

Tasted where and when:

Vintage:

Country:

Region:

Comments:

Shared with:

Served with:

Overall Rating:

Wine Name	Price

Tasted where and when:

Vintage:

Country:

Region:

Comments:

Shared with:

Served with:

Overall Rating: | | | | | | | | | | |

Wine Name	Price

Tasted where and when:

Vintage:

Country:

Region:

Comments:

Shared with:

Served with:

Overall Rating: | | | | | | | | | | |

Wine Name	Price

Tasted where and when:

Vintage:

Country:

Region:

Comments:

Shared with:

Served with:

Overall Rating: | | | | | | | | | | |

Wine Name	Price

Tasted where and when:

Vintage:

Country:

Region:

Comments:

Shared with:

Served with:

Overall Rating: | | | | | | | | | | |

Wine Name	Price

Tasted where and when:

Vintage:

Country:

Region:

Comments:

Shared with:

Served with:

Overall Rating: | | | | | | | | | | |

Wine Name	Price

Tasted where and when:

Vintage:

Country:

Region:

Comments:

Shared with:

Served with:

Overall Rating: | | | | | | | | | | |

Wine Name	Price

Tasted where and when:

Vintage:

Country:

Region:

Comments:

Shared with:

Served with:

Overall Rating: | | | | | | | | | | |

Wine Name Price

Tasted where and when:

Vintage:

Country:

Region:

Comments:

Shared with:

Served with:

Overall Rating: | | | | | | | | | | |

Wine Name	Price

Tasted where and when:

Vintage:

Country:

Region:

Comments:

Shared with:

Served with:

Overall Rating: | | | | | | | | | | |

Wine Name	Price

Tasted where and when:

Vintage:

Country:

Region:

Comments:

Shared with:

Served with:

Overall Rating: | | | | | | | | | | |

Wine Name	Price

Tasted where and when:

Vintage:

Country:

Region:

Comments:

Shared with:

Served with:

Overall Rating: | | | | | | | | | | |

Wine Name	Price

Tasted where and when:

Vintage:

Country:

Region:

Comments:

Shared with:

Served with:

Overall Rating: | | | | | | | | | | |

Wine Name	Price

Tasted where and when:

Vintage:

Country:

Region:

Comments:

Shared with:

Served with:

Overall Rating: | | | | | | | | | | |

Wine Name	Price

Tasted where and when:

Vintage:

Country:

Region:

Comments:

Shared with:

Served with:

Overall Rating: | | | | | | | | | | |

Wine Name	Price

Tasted where and when:

Vintage:

Country:

Region:

Comments:

Shared with:

Served with:

Overall Rating: | | | | | | | | | | |

Wine Name	Price

Tasted where and when:

Vintage:

Country:

Region:

Comments:

Shared with:

Served with:

Overall Rating: ☐☐☐☐☐☐☐☐☐☐

Wine Name	Price

Tasted where and when:

Vintage:

Country:

Region:

Comments:

Shared with:

Served with:

Overall Rating:

Wine Name	Price

Tasted where and when:

Vintage:

Country:

Region:

Comments:

Shared with:

Served with:

Overall Rating: | | | | | | | | | | |

Wine Name	Price

Tasted where and when:

Vintage:

Country:

Region:

Comments:

Shared with:

Served with:

Overall Rating: | | | | | | | | | | |

Wine Name	Price

Tasted where and when:

Vintage:

Country:

Region:

Comments:

Shared with:

Served with:

Overall Rating: | | | | | | | | | | |

Wine Name	Price

Tasted where and when:

Vintage:

Country:

Region:

Comments:

Shared with:

Served with:

Overall Rating: | | | | | | | | | | |

Wine Name	Price

Tasted where and when:

Vintage:

Country:

Region:

Comments:

Shared with:

Served with:

Overall Rating: | | | | | | | | | | |

Wine Name	Price

Tasted where and when:

Vintage:

Country:

Region:

Comments:

Shared with:

Served with:

Overall Rating: | | | | | | | | | | |

Wine Name	Price

Tasted where and when:

Vintage:

Country:

Region:

Comments:

Shared with:

Served with:

Overall Rating: | | | | | | | | | | |

Wine Name	Price

Tasted where and when:

Vintage:

Country:

Region:

Comments:

Shared with:

Served with:

Overall Rating: | | | | | | | | | | |

Wine Name	Price

Tasted where and when:

Vintage:

Country:

Region:

Comments:

Shared with:

Served with:

Overall Rating: ☐☐☐☐☐☐☐☐☐☐

Wine Name	Price

Tasted where and when:

Vintage:

Country:

Region:

Comments:

Shared with:

Served with:

Overall Rating: | | | | | | | | | | |

Wine Name	Price

Tasted where and when:

Vintage:

Country:

Region:

Comments:

Shared with:

Served with:

Overall Rating: | | | | | | | | | | |

Wine Name	Price

Tasted where and when:

Vintage:

Country:

Region:

Comments:

Shared with:

Served with:

Overall Rating: | | | | | | | | | | |

Wine Name	Price

Tasted where and when:

Vintage:

Country:

Region:

Comments:

Shared with:

Served with:

Overall Rating: | | | | | | | | | | |

Wine Name	Price

Tasted where and when:

Vintage:

Country:

Region:

Comments:

Shared with:

Served with:

Overall Rating: | | | | | | | | | | |

Wine Name Price

Tasted where and when:

Vintage:

Country:

Region:

Comments:

Shared with:

Served with:

Overall Rating: | | | | | | | | | | |

Wine Name	Price

Tasted where and when:

Vintage:

Country:
Region:

Comments:

Shared with:

Served with:

Overall Rating:

Wine Name	Price

Tasted where and when:

Vintage:

Country:

Region:

Comments:

Shared with:

Served with:

Overall Rating: | | | | | | | | | | |

Wine Name	Price

Tasted where and when:

Vintage:

Country:

Region:

Comments:

Shared with:

Served with:

Overall Rating: ☐☐☐☐☐☐☐☐☐☐

Wine Name	Price

Tasted where and when:

Vintage:

Country:

Region:

Comments:

Shared with:

Served with:

Overall Rating: | | | | | | | | | | |

Wine Name	Price

Tasted where and when:

Vintage:

Country:

Region:

Comments:

Shared with:

Served with:

Overall Rating: | | | | | | | | | | |
|---|---|---|---|---|---|---|---|---|---|

Wine Name	Price

Tasted where and when:

Vintage:

Country:

Region:

Comments:

Shared with:

Served with:

Overall Rating: ☐☐☐☐☐☐☐☐☐☐

Wine Name	Price

Tasted where and when:

Vintage:

Country:

Region:

Comments:

Shared with:

Served with:

Overall Rating: ☐☐☐☐☐☐☐☐☐☐

Wine Name	Price

Tasted where and when:

Vintage:

Country:

Region:

Comments:

Shared with:

Served with:

Overall Rating: | | | | | | | | | | |

Wine Name	Price

Tasted where and when:

Vintage:

Country:

Region:

Comments:

Shared with:

Served with:

Overall Rating:

Wine Name	Price

Tasted where and when:

Vintage:

Country:

Region:

Comments:

Shared with:

Served with:

Overall Rating: ☐☐☐☐☐☐☐☐☐☐

Wine Name	Price

Tasted where and when:

Vintage:

Country:

Region:

Comments:

Shared with:

Served with:

Overall Rating: | | | | | | | | | | |

Wine Name	Price

Tasted where and when:

Vintage:

Country:

Region:

Comments:

Shared with:

Served with:

Overall Rating: | | | | | | | | | | |

Wine Name	Price

Tasted where and when:

Vintage:

Country:

Region:

Comments:

Shared with:

Served with:

Overall Rating:

Wine Name	Price

Tasted where and when:

Vintage:

Country:

Region:

Comments:

Shared with:

Served with:

Overall Rating:

Wine Name	Price

Tasted where and when:

Vintage:

Country:

Region:

Comments:

Shared with:

Served with:

Overall Rating: ☐☐☐☐☐☐☐☐☐☐

Wine Name	Price

Tasted where and when:

Vintage:

Country:

Region:

Comments:

Shared with:

Served with:

Overall Rating: | | | | | | | | | | |

Wine Name	Price

Tasted where and when:

Vintage:

Country:

Region:

Comments:

Shared with:

Served with:

Overall Rating: | | | | | | | | | | |

Wine Name	Price

Tasted where and when:

Vintage:

Country:
Region:

Comments:

Shared with:

Served with:

Overall Rating: ☐☐☐☐☐☐☐☐☐☐

Wine Name	Price

Tasted where and when:

Vintage:

Country:

Region:

Comments:

Shared with:

Served with:

Overall Rating: ☐☐☐☐☐☐☐☐☐☐

Wine Name	Price

Tasted where and when:

Vintage:

Country:

Region:

Comments:

Shared with:

Served with:

Overall Rating: | | | | | | | | | | |

Wine Name	Price

Tasted where and when:

Vintage:

Country:

Region:

Comments:

Shared with:

Served with:

Overall Rating: | | | | | | | | | | |

Wine Name	Price

Tasted where and when:

Vintage:

Country:

Region:

Comments:

Shared with:

Served with:

Overall Rating:

Wine Name	Price

Tasted where and when:

Vintage:

Country:

Region:

Comments:

Shared with:

Served with:

Overall Rating:

Wine Name	Price

Tasted where and when:

Vintage:

Country:

Region:

Comments:

Shared with:

Served with:

Overall Rating:

Wine Name	Price

Tasted where and when:

Vintage:

Country:

Region:

Comments:

Shared with:

Served with:

Overall Rating: | | | | | | | | | | |

Wine Name	Price

Tasted where and when:

Vintage:

Country:

Region:

Comments:

Shared with:

Served with:

Overall Rating: | | | | | | | | | | |

Wine Name	Price

Tasted where and when:

Vintage:

Country:

Region:

Comments:

Shared with:

Served with:

Overall Rating:

Wine Name Price

Tasted where and when:

Vintage:

Country:
Region:

Comments:

Shared with:

Served with:

Overall Rating: | | | | | | | | | |

Wine Name	Price

Tasted where and when:

Vintage:

Country:

Region:

Comments:

Shared with:

Served with:

Overall Rating: ☐☐☐☐☐☐☐☐☐☐

Wine Name	Price

Tasted where and when:

Vintage:

Country:

Region:

Comments:

Shared with:

Served with:

Overall Rating:

Wine Name	Price

Tasted where and when:

Vintage:

Country:

Region:

Comments:

Shared with:

Served with:

Overall Rating:

Wine Name	Price

Tasted where and when:

Vintage:

Country:

Region:

Comments:

Shared with:

Served with:

Overall Rating:

Wine Name	Price

Tasted where and when:

Vintage:

Country:
Region:

Comments:

Shared with:

Served with:

Overall Rating: | | | | | | | | | | |

Wine Name	Price

Tasted where and when:

Vintage:

Country:

Region:

Comments:

Shared with:

Served with:

Overall Rating:

Wine Name	Price

Tasted where and when:

Vintage:

Country:

Region:

Comments:

Shared with:

Served with:

Overall Rating: | | | | | | | | | | |

Wine Name	Price

Tasted where and when:

Vintage:

Country:

Region:

Comments:

Shared with:

Served with:

Overall Rating: ☐☐☐☐☐☐☐☐☐☐

Wine Name	Price

Tasted where and when:

Vintage:

Country:

Region:

Comments:

Shared with:

Served with:

Overall Rating: ☐☐☐☐☐☐☐☐☐☐

Wine Name	Price

Tasted where and when:

Vintage:

Country:

Region:

Comments:

Shared with:

Served with:

Overall Rating: ☐ ☐ ☐ ☐ ☐ ☐ ☐ ☐ ☐ ☐

Wine Name	Price

Tasted where and when:

Vintage:

Country:

Region:

Comments:

Shared with:

Served with:

Overall Rating:

Wine Name	Price

Tasted where and when:

Vintage:

Country:

Region:

Comments:

Shared with:

Served with:

Overall Rating: | | | | | | | | | | |

Wine Name	Price

Tasted where and when:

Vintage:

Country:

Region:

Comments:

Shared with:

Served with:

Overall Rating: | | | | | | | | | | |

Wine Name	Price

Tasted where and when:

Vintage:

Country:

Region:

Comments:

Shared with:

Served with:

Overall Rating: | | | | | | | | | | |

Wine Name	Price

Tasted where and when:

Vintage:

Country:

Region:

Comments:

Shared with:

Served with:

Overall Rating:

Wine Name	Price

Tasted where and when:

Vintage:

Country:

Region:

Comments:

Shared with:

Served with:

Overall Rating: | | | | | | | | | | |

Wine Name	Price

Tasted where and when:

Vintage:

Country:
Region:

Comments:

Shared with:

Served with:

Overall Rating: | | | | | | | | | | |

Wine Name	Price

Tasted where and when:

Vintage:

Country:

Region:

Comments:

Shared with:

Served with:

Overall Rating: | | | | | | | | | | |

Wine Name	Price

Tasted where and when:

Vintage:

Country:

Region:

Comments:

Shared with:

Served with:

Overall Rating: | | | | | | | | | | |

Wine Name	Price

Tasted where and when:

Vintage:

Country:

Region:

Comments:

Shared with:

Served with:

Overall Rating: | | | | | | | | | | |

Wine Name	Price

Tasted where and when:

Vintage:

Country:

Region:

Comments:

Shared with:

Served with:

Overall Rating: | | | | | | | | | | |

Wine Name	Price

Tasted where and when:

Vintage:

Country:

Region:

Comments:

Shared with:

Served with:

Overall Rating: | | | | | | | | | | |

Wine Name	Price

Tasted where and when:

Vintage:

Country:

Region:

Comments:

Shared with:

Served with:

Overall Rating: | | | | | | | | | | |

Wine Name	Price

Tasted where and when:

Vintage:

Country:

Region:

Comments:

Shared with:

Served with:

Overall Rating:

Wine Name	Price

Tasted where and when:

Vintage:

Country:

Region:

Comments:

Shared with:

Served with:

Overall Rating: ☐ ☐ ☐ ☐ ☐ ☐ ☐ ☐ ☐ ☐

Wine Name	Price

Tasted where and when:

Vintage:

Country:

Region:

Comments:

Shared with:

Served with:

Overall Rating:

Wine Name	Price

Tasted where and when:

Vintage:

Country:

Region:

Comments:

Shared with:

Served with:

Overall Rating: | | | | | | | | | | |

Wine Name	Price

Tasted where and when:

Vintage:

Country:

Region:

Comments:

Shared with:

Served with:

Overall Rating: ☐☐☐☐☐☐☐☐☐☐

Wine Name	Price

Tasted where and when:

Vintage:

Country:

Region:

Comments:

Shared with:

Served with:

Overall Rating: ☐☐☐☐☐☐☐☐☐☐

Wine Name	Price

Tasted where and when:

Vintage:

Country:

Region:

Comments:

Shared with:

Served with:

Overall Rating: | | | | | | | | | | |

Wine Name	Price

Tasted where and when:

Vintage:

Country:

Region:

Comments:

Shared with:

Served with:

Overall Rating: | | | | | | | | | | |

Wine Name	Price

Tasted where and when:

Vintage:

Country:

Region:

Comments:

Shared with:

Served with:

Overall Rating: | | | | | | | | | | |

Wine Name	Price

Tasted where and when:

Vintage:

Country:

Region:

Comments:

Shared with:

Served with:

Overall Rating: | | | | | | | | | | |

Wine Name	Price

Tasted where and when:

Vintage:

Country:

Region:

Comments:

Shared with:

Served with:

Overall Rating:

Wine Name	Price

Tasted where and when:

Vintage:

Country:

Region:

Comments:

Shared with:

Served with:

Overall Rating: | | | | | | | | | | |

Wine Name	Price

Tasted where and when:

Vintage:

Country:

Region:

Comments:

Shared with:

Served with:

Overall Rating:

Wine Name	Price

Tasted where and when:

Vintage:

Country:

Region:

Comments:

Shared with:

Served with:

Overall Rating: | | | | | | | | | | |

Wine Name	Price

Tasted where and when:

Vintage:

Country:

Region:

Comments:

Shared with:

Served with:

Overall Rating: | | | | | | | | | | |

Wine Name Price

Tasted where and when:

Vintage:

Country:

Region:

Comments:

Shared with:

Served with:

Overall Rating: | | | | | | | | | |

Wine Name	Price

Tasted where and when:

Vintage:

Country:

Region:

Comments:

Shared with:

Served with:

Overall Rating:

Wine Name	Price

Tasted where and when:

Vintage:

Country:

Region:

Comments:

Shared with:

Served with:

Overall Rating: | | | | | | | | | | |

Wine Name	Price

Tasted where and when:

Vintage:

Country:

Region:

Comments:

Shared with:

Served with:

Overall Rating: | | | | | | | | | | |

Wine Name	Price

Tasted where and when:

Vintage:

Country:

Region:

Comments:

Shared with:

Served with:

Overall Rating: | | | | | | | | | | |

Wine Name	Price

Tasted where and when:

Vintage:

Country:

Region:

Comments:

Shared with:

Served with:

Overall Rating:

Wine Name	Price

Tasted where and when:

Vintage:

Country:

Region:

Comments:

Shared with:

Served with:

Overall Rating: ☐☐☐☐☐☐☐☐☐☐

Wine Name	Price

Tasted where and when:

Vintage:

Country:

Region:

Comments:

Shared with:

Served with:

Overall Rating: ☐☐☐☐☐☐☐☐☐☐

Wine Name	Price

Tasted where and when:

Vintage:

Country:

Region:

Comments:

Shared with:

Served with:

Overall Rating: | | | | | | | | | | |

Wine Name	Price

Tasted where and when:

Vintage:

Country:

Region:

Comments:

Shared with:

Served with:

Overall Rating: | | | | | | | | | | |

Wine Name	Price

Tasted where and when:

Vintage:

Country:

Region:

Comments:

Shared with:

Served with:

Overall Rating:

Wine Name	Price

Tasted where and when:

Vintage:

Country:

Region:

Comments:

Shared with:

Served with:

Overall Rating: | | | | | | | | | | |

Wine Name	Price

Tasted where and when:

Vintage:

Country:

Region:

Comments:

Shared with:

Served with:

Overall Rating: | | | | | | | | | | |

Wine Name	Price

Tasted where and when:

Vintage:

Country:

Region:

Comments:

Shared with:

Served with:

Overall Rating: | | | | | | | | | | |

Wine Name	Price

Tasted where and when:

Vintage:

Country:

Region:

Comments:

Shared with:

Served with:

Overall Rating:

Wine Name	Price

Tasted where and when:

Vintage:

Country:

Region:

Comments:

Shared with:

Served with:

Overall Rating: | | | | | | | | | | |

Wine Name	Price

Tasted where and when:

Vintage:

Country:
Region:

Comments:

Shared with:

Served with:

Overall Rating: | | | | | | | | | | |

Wine Name	Price

Tasted where and when:

Vintage:

Country:

Region:

Comments:

Shared with:

Served with:

Overall Rating:

Wine Name	Price

Tasted where and when:

Vintage:

Country:

Region:

Comments:

Shared with:

Served with:

Overall Rating: | | | | | | | | | | |

Wine Name	Price

Tasted where and when:

Vintage:

Country:

Region:

Comments:

Shared with:

Served with:

Overall Rating: | | | | | | | | | | |

Wine Name	Price

Tasted where and when:

Vintage:

Country:

Region:

Comments:

Shared with:

Served with:

Overall Rating:

Wine Name	Price

Tasted where and when:

Vintage:

Country:

Region:

Comments:

Shared with:

Served with:

Overall Rating:

Wine Name	Price

Tasted where and when:

Vintage:

Country:

Region:

Comments:

Shared with:

Served with:

Overall Rating: | | | | | | | | | | |

Wine Name	Price

Tasted where and when:

Vintage:

Country:

Region:

Comments:

Shared with:

Served with:

Overall Rating: | | | | | | | | | | |

Wine Name	Price

Tasted where and when:

Vintage:

Country:
Region:

Comments:

Shared with:

Served with:

Overall Rating: | | | | | | | | | | |

Wine Name	Price

Tasted where and when:

Vintage:

Country:

Region:

Comments:

Shared with:

Served with:

Overall Rating:

Wine Name	Price

Tasted where and when:

Vintage:

Country:

Region:

Comments:

Shared with:

Served with:

Overall Rating:

Wine Name	Price

Tasted where and when:

Vintage:

Country:

Region:

Comments:

Shared with:

Served with:

Overall Rating: | | | | | | | | | | |

Wine Name	Price

Tasted where and when:

Vintage:

Country:

Region:

Comments:

Shared with:

Served with:

Overall Rating: | | | | | | | | | | |

Wine Name	Price

Tasted where and when:

Vintage:

Country:

Region:

Comments:

Shared with:

Served with:

Overall Rating:

Wine Name	Price

Tasted where and when:

Vintage:

Country:

Region:

Comments:

Shared with:

Served with:

Overall Rating: | | | | | | | | | | |

Wine Name	Price

Tasted where and when:

Vintage:

Country:

Region:

Comments:

Shared with:

Served with:

Overall Rating: | | | | | | | | | | |

Wine Name	Price

Tasted where and when:

Vintage:

Country:

Region:

Comments:

Shared with:

Served with:

Overall Rating: | | | | | | | | | | |

Wine Name	Price

Tasted where and when:

Vintage:

Country:

Region:

Comments:

Shared with:

Served with:

Overall Rating: | | | | | | | | | | |

Wine Name	Price

Tasted where and when:

Vintage:

Country:

Region:

Comments:

Shared with:

Served with:

Overall Rating: | | | | | | | | | | |

Wine Name	Price

Tasted where and when:

Vintage:

Country:

Region:

Comments:

Shared with:

Served with:

Overall Rating: | | | | | | | | | | |

Wine Name	Price

Tasted where and when:

Vintage:

Country:

Region:

Comments:

Shared with:

Served with:

Overall Rating: | | | | | | | | | | |

Wine Name	Price

Tasted where and when:

Vintage:

Country:

Region:

Comments:

Shared with:

Served with:

Overall Rating: | | | | | | | | | | |

Wine Name	Price

Tasted where and when:

Vintage:

Country:

Region:

Comments:

Shared with:

Served with:

Overall Rating: | | | | | | | | | | |

Wine Name	Price

Tasted where and when:

Vintage:

Country:

Region:

Comments:

Shared with:

Served with:

Overall Rating: | | | | | | | | | | |

Wine Name	Price

Tasted where and when:

Vintage:

Country:

Region:

Comments:

Shared with:

Served with:

Overall Rating: | | | | | | | | | | |

Wine Name	Price

Tasted where and when:

Vintage:

Country:

Region:

Comments:

Shared with:

Served with:

Overall Rating: | | | | | | | | | | |

Wine Name	Price

Tasted where and when:

Vintage:

Country:

Region:

Comments:

Shared with:

Served with:

Overall Rating: | | | | | | | | | | |

Wine Name	Price

Tasted where and when:

Vintage:

Country:
Region:

Comments:

Shared with:

Served with:

Overall Rating:

Wine Name	Price

Tasted where and when:

Vintage:

Country:

Region:

Comments:

Shared with:

Served with:

Overall Rating: ☐☐☐☐☐☐☐☐☐☐

Wine Name	Price

Tasted where and when:

Vintage:

Country:

Region:

Comments:

Shared with:

Served with:

Overall Rating: | | | | | | | | | | |

Wine Name	Price

Tasted where and when:

Vintage:

Country:

Region:

Comments:

Shared with:

Served with:

Overall Rating: | | | | | | | | | | |

Wine Name	Price

Tasted where and when:

Vintage:

Country:

Region:

Comments:

Shared with:

Served with:

Overall Rating: | | | | | | | | | | |

Wine Name	Price

Tasted where and when:

Vintage:

Country:

Region:

Comments:

Shared with:

Served with:

Overall Rating:

Wine Name	Price

Tasted where and when:

Vintage:

Country:

Region:

Comments:

Shared with:

Served with:

Overall Rating: | | | | | | | | | | |

Wine Name	Price

Tasted where and when:

Vintage:

Country:

Region:

Comments:

Shared with:

Served with:

Overall Rating: ☐☐☐☐☐☐☐☐☐☐

Wine Name	Price

Tasted where and when:

Vintage:

Country:

Region:

Comments:

Shared with:

Served with:

Overall Rating: | | | | | | | | | | |

Wine Name	Price

Tasted where and when:

Vintage:

Country:

Region:

Comments:

Shared with:

Served with:

Overall Rating: | | | | | | | | | | |

Wine Name	Price

Tasted where and when:

Vintage:

Country:

Region:

Comments:

Shared with:

Served with:

Overall Rating:

Wine Name	Price

Tasted where and when:

Vintage:

Country:

Region:

Comments:

Shared with:

Served with:

Overall Rating: ☐☐☐☐☐☐☐☐☐☐

Wine Name	Price

Tasted where and when:

Vintage:

Country:
Region:

Comments:

Shared with:

Served with:

Overall Rating: | | | | | | | | | | |

Wine Name	Price

Tasted where and when:

Vintage:

Country:

Region:

Comments:

Shared with:

Served with:

Overall Rating: | | | | | | | | | | |

Wine Name	Price

Tasted where and when:

Vintage:

Country:

Region:

Comments:

Shared with:

Served with:

Overall Rating:

Wine Name	Price

Tasted where and when:

Vintage:

Country:

Region:

Comments:

Shared with:

Served with:

Overall Rating: | | | | | | | | | | |

Wine Name	Price

Tasted where and when:

Vintage:

Country:

Region:

Comments:

Shared with:

Served with:

Overall Rating: | | | | | | | | | | |

Wine Name	Price

Tasted where and when:

Vintage: Country:

Region:

Comments:

Shared with: Served with:

Overall Rating: | | | | | | | | | | |

Wine Name	Price

Tasted where and when:

Vintage:

Country:

Region:

Comments:

Shared with:

Served with:

Overall Rating: | | | | | | | | | | |

Wine Name	Price

Tasted where and when:

Vintage:

Country:

Region:

Comments:

Shared with:

Served with:

Overall Rating: | | | | | | | | | | |

Wine Name	Price

Tasted where and when:

Vintage:

Country:

Region:

Comments:

Shared with:

Served with:

Overall Rating: | | | | | | | | | | |

Wine Name	Price

Tasted where and when:

Vintage:

Country:

Region:

Comments:

Shared with:

Served with:

Overall Rating: | | | | | | | | | | |

Wine Name	Price

Tasted where and when:

Vintage:

Country:

Region:

Comments:

Shared with:

Served with:

Overall Rating:

Wine Name	Price

Tasted where and when:

Vintage:

Country:

Region:

Comments:

Shared with:

Served with:

Overall Rating: | | | | | | | | | | |

Wine Name	Price

Tasted where and when:

Vintage:

Country:

Region:

Comments:

Shared with:

Served with:

Overall Rating: | | | | | | | | | | |

Wine Name	Price

Tasted where and when:

Vintage:

Country:

Region:

Comments:

Shared with:

Served with:

Overall Rating:

Wine Name	Price

Tasted where and when:

Vintage:

Country:

Region:

Comments:

Shared with:

Served with:

Overall Rating: | | | | | | | | | | |

Wine Name	Price

Tasted where and when:

Vintage:

Country:

Region:

Comments:

Shared with:

Served with:

Overall Rating: | | | | | | | | | | |

Wine Name	Price

Tasted where and when:

Vintage:

Country:

Region:

Comments:

Shared with:

Served with:

Overall Rating: ☐☐☐☐☐☐☐☐☐☐

Wine Name	Price

Tasted where and when:

Vintage:

Country:

Region:

Comments:

Shared with:

Served with:

Overall Rating: | | | | | | | | | | |

Wine Name	Price

Tasted where and when:

Vintage:

Country:

Region:

Comments:

Shared with:

Served with:

Overall Rating: | | | | | | | | | | |

Wine Name	Price

Tasted where and when:

Vintage:

Country:

Region:

Comments:

Shared with:

Served with:

Overall Rating: | | | | | | | | | | |

Wine Name	Price

Tasted where and when:

Vintage:

Country:

Region:

Comments:

Shared with:

Served with:

Overall Rating:

Wine Name	Price

Tasted where and when:

Vintage:

Country:

Region:

Comments:

Shared with:

Served with:

Overall Rating: | | | | | | | | | | |

Wine Name	Price

Tasted where and when:

Vintage:

Country:

Region:

Comments:

Shared with:

Served with:

Overall Rating: | | | | | | | | | | |

Wine Name	Price

Tasted where and when:

Vintage:

Country:

Region:

Comments:

Shared with:

Served with:

Overall Rating:

Wine Name	Price

Tasted where and when:

Vintage:

Country:

Region:

Comments:

Shared with:

Served with:

Overall Rating: | | | | | | | | | | |

Wine Name	Price

Tasted where and when:

Vintage:

Country:

Region:

Comments:

Shared with:

Served with:

Overall Rating: ☐☐☐☐☐☐☐☐☐☐

Wine Name	Price

Tasted where and when:

Vintage:

Country:

Region:

Comments:

Shared with:

Served with:

Overall Rating: ☐☐☐☐☐☐☐☐☐☐

Wine Name	Price

Tasted where and when:

Vintage:

Country:

Region:

Comments:

Shared with:

Served with:

Overall Rating: | | | | | | | | | | |

Wine Name	Price

Tasted where and when:

Vintage:

Country:

Region:

Comments:

Shared with:

Served with:

Overall Rating: ☐☐☐☐☐☐☐☐☐☐

Wine Name	Price

Tasted where and when:

Vintage:

Country:

Region:

Comments:

Shared with:

Served with:

Overall Rating:

Wine Name	Price

Tasted where and when:

Vintage:

Country:

Region:

Comments:

Shared with:

Served with:

Overall Rating: | | | | | | | | | | |

Wine Name	Price

Tasted where and when:

Vintage:

Country:

Region:

Comments:

Shared with:

Served with:

Overall Rating: | | | | | | | | | | |

Wine Name	Price

Tasted where and when:

Vintage:

Country:

Region:

Comments:

Shared with:

Served with:

Overall Rating: | | | | | | | | | | |

Wine Name	Price

Tasted where and when:

Vintage:

Country:

Region:

Comments:

Shared with:

Served with:

Overall Rating:

Wine Name	Price

Tasted where and when:

Vintage:

Country:

Region:

Comments:

Shared with:

Served with:

Overall Rating: | | | | | | | | | | |

Wine Name	Price

Tasted where and when:

Vintage:

Country:

Region:

Comments:

Shared with:

Served with:

Overall Rating: | | | | | | | | | | |

Wine Name	Price

Tasted where and when:

Vintage:

Country:

Region:

Comments:

Shared with:

Served with:

Overall Rating: | | | | | | | | | | |

Wine Name	Price

Tasted where and when:

Vintage:

Country:

Region:

Comments:

Shared with:

Served with:

Overall Rating: | | | | | | | | | | |

Wine Name	Price

Tasted where and when:

Vintage:

Country:

Region:

Comments:

Shared with:

Served with:

Overall Rating: ☐☐☐☐☐☐☐☐☐☐

Wine Name	Price

Tasted where and when:

Vintage:

Country:

Region:

Comments:

Shared with:

Served with:

Overall Rating: | | | | | | | | | | |

Wine Name	Price

Tasted where and when:

Vintage:

Country:

Region:

Comments:

Shared with:

Served with:

Overall Rating: | | | | | | | | | | |

Wine Name	Price

Tasted where and when:

Vintage:

Country:

Region:

Comments:

Shared with:

Served with:

Overall Rating: | | | | | | | | | | |

Wine Name	Price

Tasted where and when:

Vintage:

Country:

Region:

Comments:

Shared with:

Served with:

Overall Rating: | | | | | | | | | | |

Wine Name	Price

Tasted where and when:

Vintage:

Country:

Region:

Comments:

Shared with:

Served with:

Overall Rating:

Wine Name	Price

Tasted where and when:

Vintage:

Country:

Region:

Comments:

Shared with:

Served with:

Overall Rating: | | | | | | | | | | |

Wine Name	Price

Tasted where and when:

Vintage:

Country:

Region:

Comments:

Shared with:

Served with:

Overall Rating: | | | | | | | | | | |

Wine Name	Price

Tasted where and when:

Vintage:

Country:

Region:

Comments:

Shared with:

Served with:

Overall Rating: ☐☐☐☐☐☐☐☐☐☐

Wine Name	Price

Tasted where and when:

Vintage:

Country:

Region:

Comments:

Shared with:

Served with:

Overall Rating: ☐☐☐☐☐☐☐☐☐☐

Wine Name	Price

Tasted where and when:

Vintage:

Country:

Region:

Comments:

Shared with:

Served with:

Overall Rating: ☐☐☐☐☐☐☐☐☐☐

Wine Name	Price

Tasted where and when:

Vintage:

Country:

Region:

Comments:

Shared with:

Served with:

Overall Rating: ☐☐☐☐☐☐☐☐☐☐

Wine Name	Price

Tasted where and when:

Vintage:

Country:

Region:

Comments:

Shared with:

Served with:

Overall Rating: | | | | | | | | | | |

Wine Name	Price

Tasted where and when:

Vintage:

Country:

Region:

Comments:

Shared with:

Served with:

Overall Rating:

Wine Name	Price

Tasted where and when:

Vintage:

Country:

Region:

Comments:

Shared with:

Served with:

Overall Rating: | | | | | | | | | | |

Wine Name	Price

Tasted where and when:

Vintage:

Country:

Region:

Comments:

Shared with:

Served with:

Overall Rating: | | | | | | | | | | |

Wine Name Price

Tasted where and when:

Vintage:

Country:

Region:

Comments:

Shared with:

Served with:

Overall Rating: | | | | | | | | | |

Wine Name	Price

Tasted where and when:

Vintage:

Country:

Region:

Comments:

Shared with:

Served with:

Overall Rating: | | | | | | | | | | |

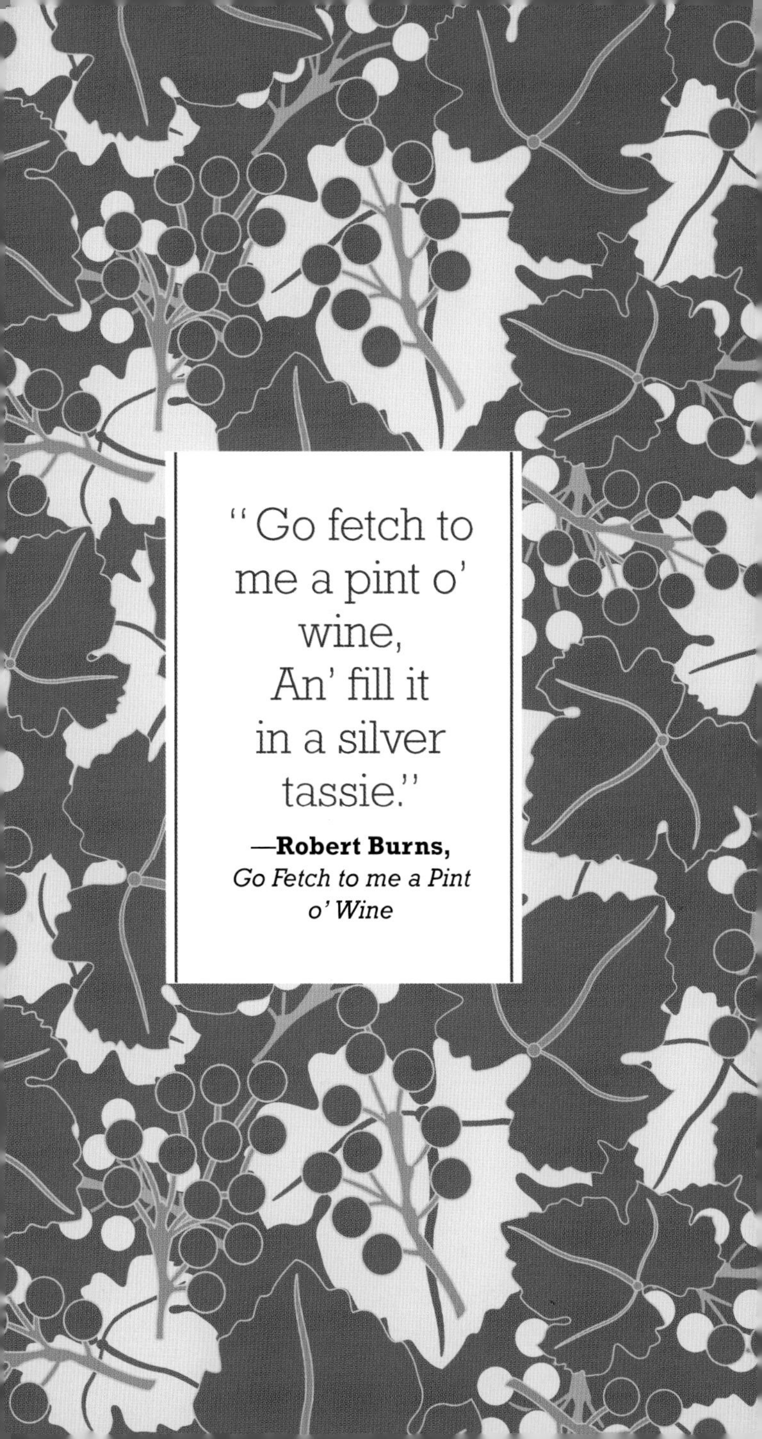
"Go fetch to me a pint o' wine,
An' fill it in a silver tassie."
—Robert Burns,
Go Fetch to me a Pint o' Wine